PRACTISE TOGETHER SERIES

SPELLING

Denis Ballance

A Piccolo Original
Piccolo Books

A note to parents

This book is designed for children between 7-10+ years to practise their spelling.

Good spelling involves 'seeing' the word in the mind and translating this accurately into writing. The sound of the word, which helps good reading, is not as important for accurate spelling, so words should be looked at and then written down, rather than sounded out. (You check if you've spelt something correctly by writing it and looking at it, not saying it.) It is therefore important to practise spelling in the following sequence:

- look at the word
- cover it and conjur up its shape, its word-picture
- write it down
- check it

As the 'shape' of words can help fix the correct spelling, wherever possible words with the same shape (but which don't necessarily have to sound the same) should be grouped together, e.g. thought, bough, rough.

This book practises spelling in this way, encouraging the child to look at groups of words which contain similar letter patterns, or which are on the same theme (e.g. sport), copy them accurately, then write them in context. There are also puzzles and wordgames for motivation and to give further practice.

The activities in the book encourage children to work at their own pace. Occasionally they may ask for help – don't give the answer right away but use questions to encourage the child to find the solution alone and give plenty of praise.

The pages can be done in any order. Some may be slightly more difficult than others, so don't let the child get bogged down. The activities are there to be enjoyed. When they stop being fun, it is time for a rest and a change. So encourage the child to work in short bursts and don't let the exercises become a chore.

The parent notes on some of the pages give useful advice about the activities if you wish to work more closely with the child. (In order to avoid using 'he/she, him/her' in this book, we have referred to the child as 'he' in these notes).

The work is presented in a form which children should find interesting and enjoyable. It will be all the more enjoyable and valuable if you are willing to become actively involved in what your child is doing. The puzzles and activities should provide considerable motivation in themselves, but this motivation will be greatly enhanced by your encouragement, interest and – above all – praise.

All the answers can be found on pages 31 and 32.

Look/Cover	Write
there	
who	
came	
was	was
what	what
have	
some	
come	
made	
right	

1 Write the word again in this poem.

Along our street There lived a man
Who was known as Mixed Up Dan.
One day he come to buy some gold
For that Was what my father sold.
I said to him "what lack of shame!,
Why do you have such a funny name?"
"Spelling," he said, "no problem for Some
But, as for me, it just won't come!
I've made an effort, but hard as I fight,
I mix up the letters – just can't get it r."

2 Sometimes, Mixed Up Dan gets all the letters in the wrong order and spells his name AND instead of DAN. Which words is he trying to spell here?

(1) how who
(2) saw was
(3) dame made
(4) thaw what
(5) mace came

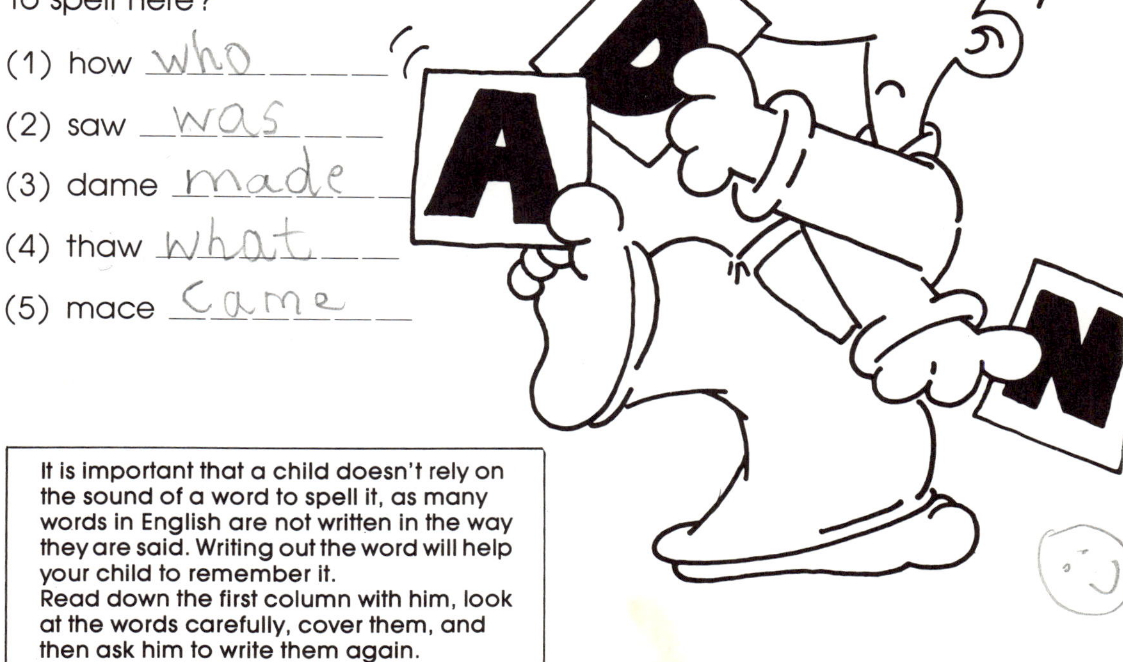

It is important that a child doesn't rely on the sound of a word to spell it, as many words in English are not written in the way they are said. Writing out the word will help your child to remember it.
Read down the first column with him, look at the words carefully, cover them, and then ask him to write them again.

Look/Cover	Write
two	
which	
from	
were	
said	
their	
could	
about	
before	
little	

1

Write words from the list in this puzzle. Follow the direction of the arrow,

What grows on the tree?

2

Mixed Up Dan is in trouble again! He has got his letters in the wrong order. Which words from the list above is he trying to spell here?

(1) cwhhi ___________

(2) eitltl ___________

(3) roebfe ___________

(4) rewe ___________

These copy, cover and write activities will help reinforce the 'shape' of the word in the child's mind and will lead to accurate spelling.

Look/ Cover	Write
went	________
our	________
where	________
like	________
only	________
one	________
when	________
want	________
with	________
other	________

1 Write the word again in the sentence.

We ________ to Margate last year.

I see ________ postman every day.

________ does Mrs Hammond live?

I ________ lollypops and sweets.

The car is ________ one year old.

There is only ________ sweet left.

________ are you coming round to play?

Do you ________ to ride my bicycle?

I went to stay ________ Uncle Peter.

The ________ girls like skating.

2 Use the words from the list above to complete the story.
Tick the words off in the boxes as you use them.

(1) ________ house is near the zoo. Last week, we (2) ________ there for the day. We (3) ________ the brown bears best. The place (4) ________ they are kept is very big. There were (5) ________ two bears out in the open run. The (6) ________ bear was inside the pen. He did not (7) ________ to come out. Dad said he would come outside (8) ________ he was hungry. (9) ________ of the other bears went inside. Soon, the third bear came out (10) ________ him and they began to play.

Look, cover and then write.

fork	________	north	________	corgi	________
door	________	sword	________	shorts	________
horn	________	horse	________	mirror	________
fort	________	sport	________	anorak	________

The answers to this puzzle are all in the list of words above. With the help of the picture clues, write the correct word in each space. If your answers are correct, the down column will spell the name of a sea creature.

In the list above are words with the same letter pattern – all the words contain the letter string 'or'. It often helps a child with spelling if words with the same letter strings are grouped together. When you've worked through the examples on the page, try together to think of other words with the 'or' letter string.

Look/Cover/Write	Look	Write again	√ or self correct
ear ________			
neat ________			
pear ________			
year ________	85/86		
heap ________			
beat ________			
meat ________			
seat ________			
leaf ________			
head ________			

Make your own '__ea__' words by writing the missing letters.
Say each word.

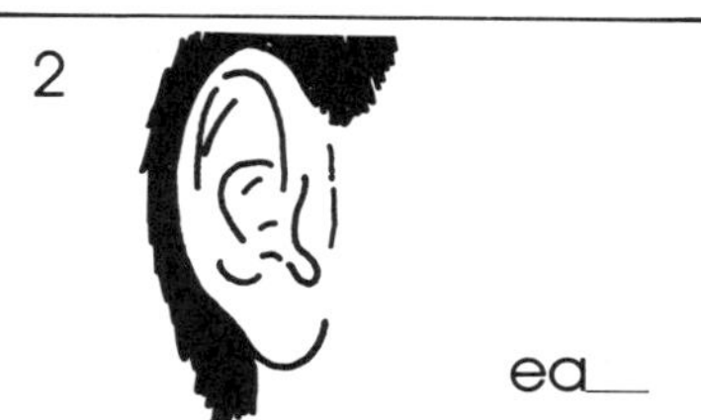

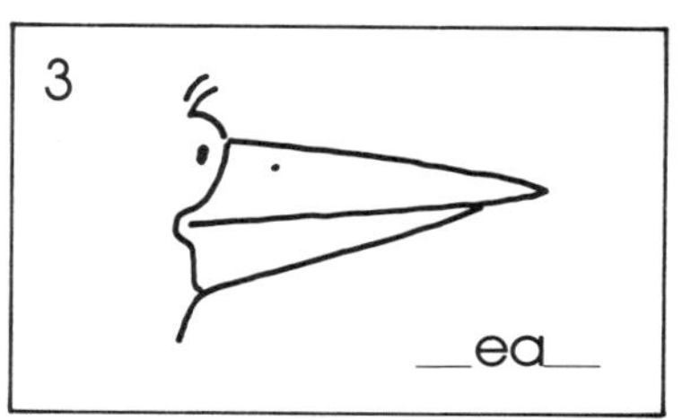

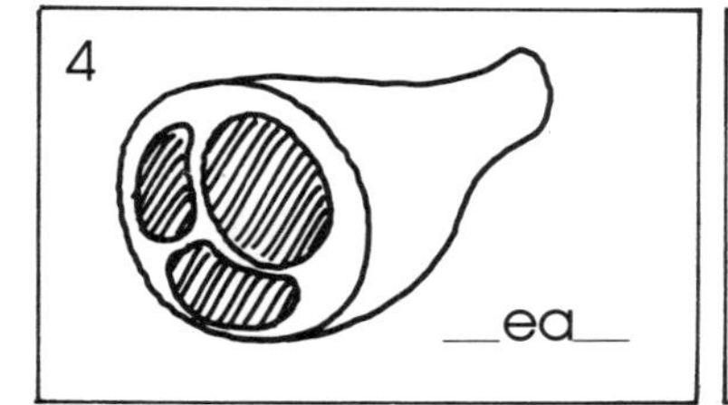

All the words in the list above contain the letter string 'ea'. Read down the first column with the child. Wrong spellings should be self-corrected in the fourth column.

Look, cover and then write.

bear ________	camel ________	rabbit ________
lion ________	tiger ________	elephant ________
wolf ________	badger ________	leopard ________
panda ________	monkey ________	giraffe ________

1

Find the animal names from the list which are hidden in these sentences.

Example Don't be a roamer. Don't be a roamer. be a r bear

(1) He won a badge recently.

(2) They always came late.

(3) She has a shop and a stall.

(4) Is she the girl I once knew?

2

Can you complete these animal rhymes with words from the list?

(1) It isn't very fair

To stare at a ________

(2) One shouldn't laugh

At the stately ________

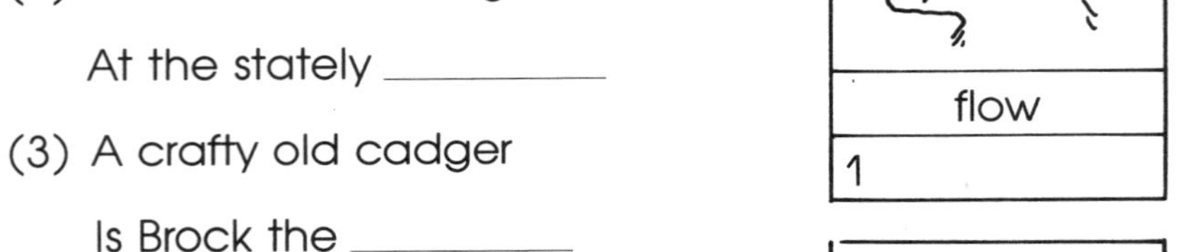

(3) A crafty old cadger

Is Brock the ________

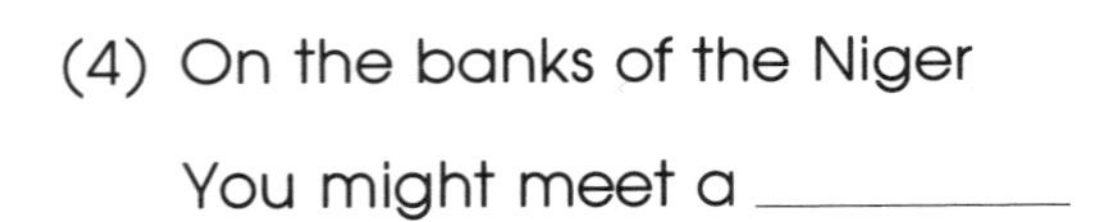

(4) On the banks of the Niger

You might meet a ________

(5) No friend of the shepherd

Is the wild spotted ________

3

Mixed Up Dan has been painting names on the animals' pens. Can you put them right for him?

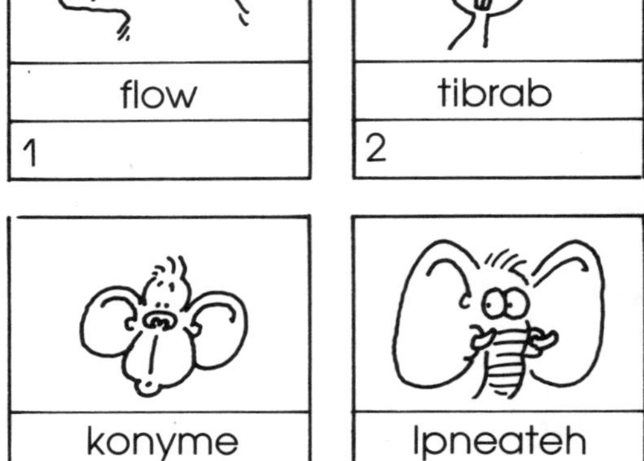

The theme of the list on this page is animals. The exercises and puzzles will help to fix the correct letter sequences in your child's mind.

Look, cover and then write.

red	________	brown	________	blue	________	cream	________
pink	________	black	________	grey	________	yellow	________
white	________	lemon	________	green	________	purple	________

1

Colour these flags.
Use two different colours for each flag and write their names underneath.

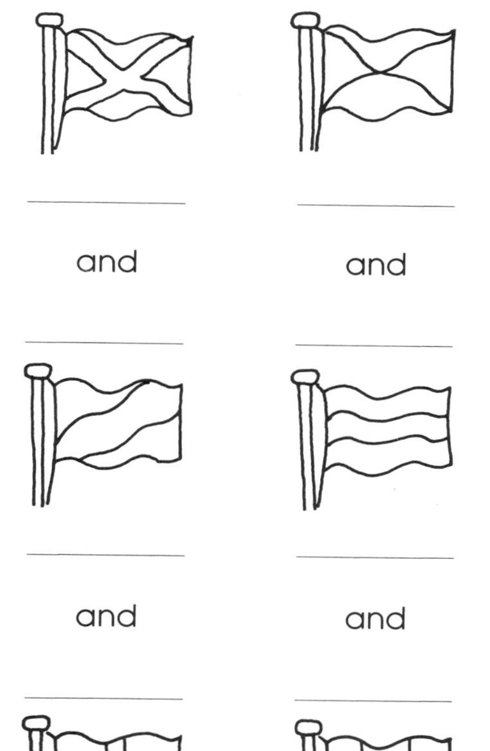

2

Fill in the missing words to complete this crossword puzzle. The answers are all names of colours from the list.

The theme of the list on this page is colours. Ask the child to copy the words out first before tackling the exercises.

Look/Cover	Write
saw	_______
sore	_______
wood	_______
would	_______
flour	_______
flower	_______
board	_______
bored	_______
hare	_______
hair	_______
new	_______
knew	_______

1 Write the word again in the sentence.

I _______ you playing in the park.

Jackie had a very _______ finger.

Dad's new shed is made of _______ .

Mark _______ like to join the club.

Most wheat is ground into _______ .

Anne wore a _______ on her dress.

Tom mended the fence with a _______ .

I was _______ with the television.

The _______ ran across the fields.

Lorna's _______ is fine and soft.

I needed a _______ exercise book.

Everybody _______ where you were.

2 Write a word from the list in each space and under each picture.

The red fox lay at the edge of the (1) _______ . Her feet were (2) _______ and she (3) _______ that the hunt (4) _______ be on her trail. She yawned, as though (5) _______ with the whole affair and set off to lead the hounds away from her (6) _______ cubs.

Children often confuse words which sound the same but are spelt differently. Words of this kind are called homophones. 'Saw' and 'sore' are not strictly homophones but sometimes cause difficulties.

Look/Cover	Write
peace	____________
piece	____________
rode	____________
road	____________
meter	____________
metre	____________
tire	____________
tyre	____________
way	____________
weigh	____________
draw	____________
drawer	____________

1 Write the word again in the sentence.

Christmas is a time of ____________ and joy.

I should like a smaller ____________ of cake.

Maria ____________ down the hill far too fast.

Is this the main ____________ to Cambridge?

The man came to read the gas ____________ .

Ask the lady for a ____________ of pink felt.

Andrew never seems to ____________ of fishing.

The car needs a new ____________ .

Gareth runs all the ____________ to school.

The ticket checker will ____________ your case.

Ask Sam to ____________ a plan of the garden.

You will find the letters in the top ____________

2 Choose the best word from the list to match each picture.

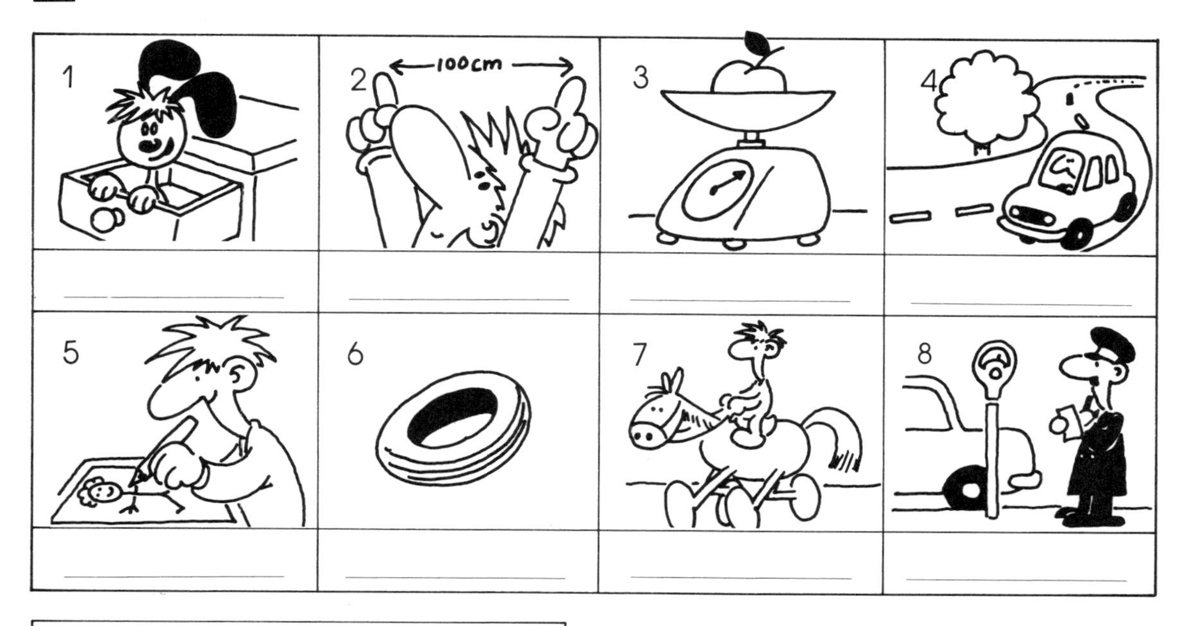

'Draw' and 'drawer' are not homophones but they are often confused.

Look, cover and then write.

apple	________	cherry	________	pea	________
cabbage	________	pineapple	________	banana	________
potato	________	orange	________	plum	________
peach	________	carrot	________	grape	________

1 Write the correct name under each picture. Cover the list.

2 Change one letter to make these words into the names of fruits from the list. Write your answers under the words.

glum perch sherry grate

(1) ________ (2) ________ (3) ________ (4) ________

3 Complete this crossword with names of fruits and vegetables from the list.

1 b	2 s	3 l	4 p	5 s	6 s	7 s
8 r	h	e		9 p	t	t
o	e	10 g	a	e	e	o
11 a	a	a		12 c	e	r
d	k	l	h	k	l	y

The theme of the list on this page is fruit and vegetables. Ask the child to copy the list of words before tackling the exercises.

1 Write the plurals of these words.

(1) bus ______ (4) cross ______ (7) church ______

(2) tax ______ (5) bush ______ (8) patch ______

(3) class ______ (6) fox ______

2 Write the plurals of the words in this box to fill the spaces in the story.

bush	woman	patch	
card	witch	dress	branch
wish	box	trick	

Mixed Up Dan was out in the woods when he met two poor old (1) w ______ gathering bundles of sticks. Their (2) d ______ were torn and covered in (3) p ______ .

Dan offered to help.

When he had gathered a pile of (4) b ______ , the older woman said, "You have been kind to us. We are (5) w ______ and we should like to give you one of our (6) w ______ ."

"Please turn me into a good speller," Dan said.

The witch smiled at him sadly and said, "We are not allowed to tell you our secret spells, but we can give you some magic. It is in two (7) b ______ which are hidden behind those (8) b ______ ." Eagerly, Dan opened the boxes. Inside the first were two packs of (9) c ______ . The other held a book called 'My First Book of Easy Card (10) T ______ '.

> A noun ending in '- s', '- ss', '-ch', '-sh', or 'x' adds '-es' to form its plural. **Example:** gas - gases, glass - glasses, watch - watches, sash - sashes, box - boxes. There are very few exceptions to this rule. Check your child understands the meaning of **plural** before starting this page.

Look/Cover/Write	Look	Write again	√ or self correct
arm ________			
card ________	HAPPY BIRTH DAY		
farm ________			
garden ________			
jar ________			
star ________			
scarf ________			
car ________			
bark ________			
shark ________			
caravan ________			

Use words from the list to fill the spaces in these sentences.

Old Tom Ross lives in a (1) ________ on a (2) ________ near the village. Although he has only one (3) ________ he looks after the farmer's vegetable (4) ________ . Everyone on the farm likes Old Tom. When he drives his (5) ________ into the yard even the dogs (6) ________ and jump for joy.

> All the words in the list above contain the letter string 'ar'. When you've worked through the exercises on the page, try together to think of other words with the 'ar' letter string.

Look/Cover	Write
milk	
chips	
bread	
cheese	
pizza	
potato	
coffee	
biscuit	
sausages	
chocolate	
hamburger	
ice-cream	

1 Write the correct word under each picture.

2 Mixed Up Dan has lost all his consonants. Can you complete these words for him? They are all from the list above.

(1) _ i _ _ u i _ (5) i _ e - _ _ e a _ (9) _ _ i _ _

(2) _ o _ _ e e (6) _ a _ _ u _ _ e _ (10) _ _ o _ o _ a _ e

(3) _ o _ a _ o (7) _ i _ _ (11) _ a u _ a _ e _

(4) _ _ e a _ (8) _ i _ _ a (12) _ _ e e _ e

Before the child starts the second exercise, make sure he knows the difference between a vowel (a,o,u,i,e), and a consonant (s,t,d,p etc). All the words are taken from the above list.

Look, cover and then write.

pin	pinned	pinning	stop	stopped	stopping
hop	hopped	hopping	drop	dropped	dropping
tap	tapped	tapping	skip	skipped	skipping
pat	patted	patting	drag	dragged	dragging
shop	shopped	shopping	chop	chopped	chopping
step	stepped	stepping	slip	slipped	slipping

Can you help Mixed Up Dan complete these sets of words?

(1) slap ________ ________

(2) grip ________ ________

(3) chat ________ ________

(4) snip ________ ________

The list above contains verbs which double the last consonant to form the past tense and the present participle. See if the child notices the pattern, and together try to think of other words which follow the same pattern. (There are exceptions!)

Look/Cover/Write	Look	Write again	√ or self correct
bone ________			
cake ________			
face ________			
five ________			
gate ________			
hole ________			
nine ________			
rake ________			
pipe ________			
rose ________			
spade ________			
smoke ________			

Write each word and add a magic 'e'. Say both words.

rip	________	pin	________	rat	________
fat	________	hop	________	bit	________
can	________	hat	________	tap	________
not	________	kit	________	din	________

The list above contains words where the final 'e' lengthens the sound of the preceding vowel, often called 'Magic E words'. (The preceding vowel is pronounced like the name sound of the letter, eg rake, the 'a' is pronounced 'ay' like the letter 'a'.) Work through the exercises, and when the child has completed them perhaps together you can think of other 'Magic E words'.

1 Make a pattern by colouring all the boxes which contain a word ending in a consonant + 'y'.

fly	pony	lorry	baby	cry
journey	country	jelly	trolley	
day	valley	berry	cowboy	toy
pulley	library	hobby	alley	
key	pantry	canary	poppy	bay

2 Write the plurals of these words into the spaces to complete the story.

baby toy
sty mystery cherry
puppy collie day pansy
daisy lady

Carol had two (1) p __________ . They were black and white (2) c __________ .

While they were (3) b __________ , they were very well behaved but after a while, Carol noticed that some of her (4) t __________ were starting to disappear.

There were other (5) m __________ too. Carol's mother lost a bowl which had been full of (6) c __________ . Strange things began to happen in the garden. Carol's father sowed some (7) p __________ and (8) d __________ in a seed box. The next morning, they were nowhere to be found.

A few (9) d __________ later, one of the (10) l __________ from the farm next door caught the culprits in the act. She saw the (11) p __________ dragging something through the hedge. When she went to see what they were doing, she found a doll which they were burying and all the lost things behind the pig (12) s __________ .

Family→ families. To form the plural of a word ending in a consonant + y, change the 'y' to 'ies'.
Key→keys. To form the plural of a word ending in a vowel + y, just add 's'.

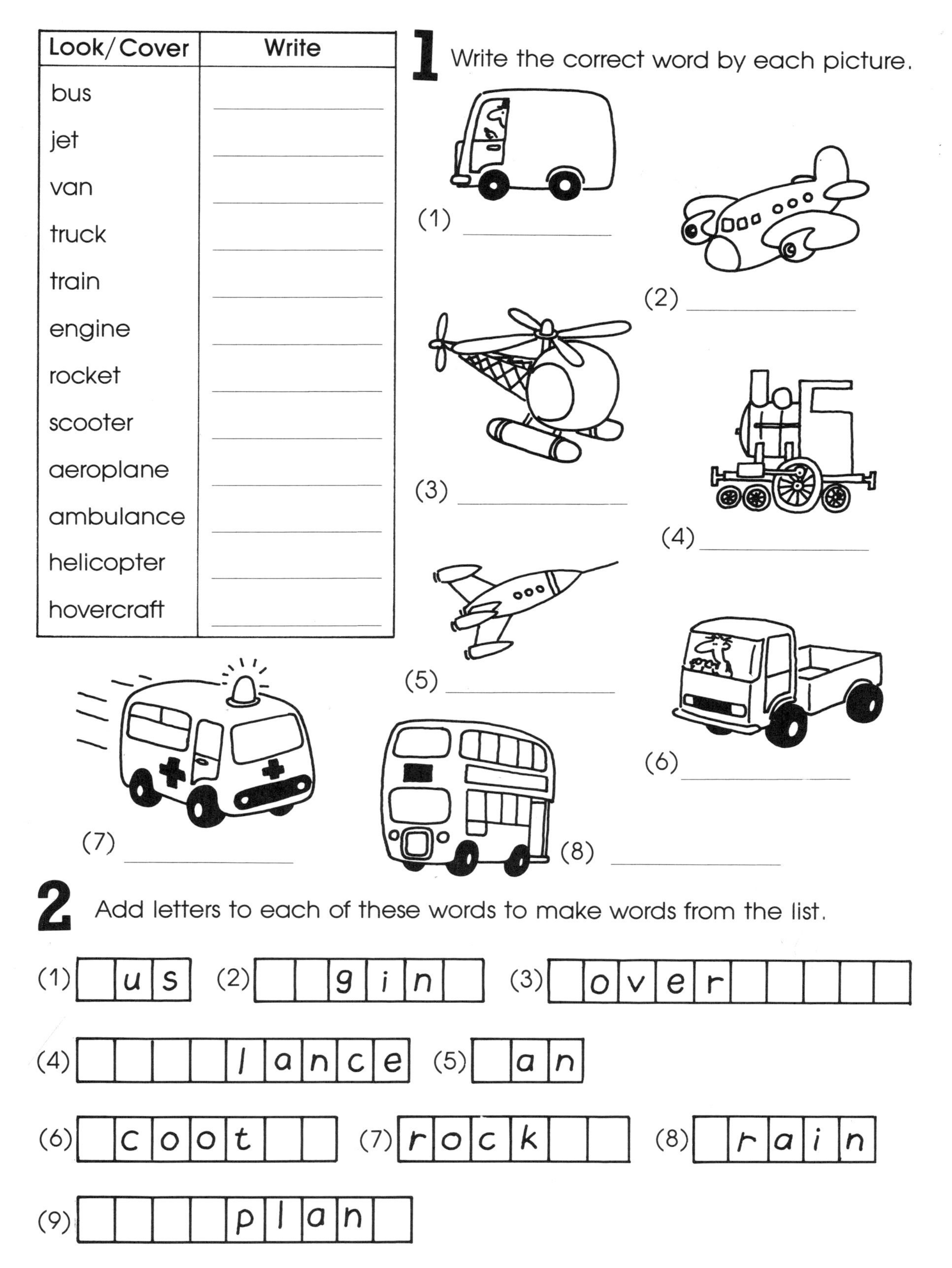

Look/Cover	Write
bus	
jet	
van	
truck	
train	
engine	
rocket	
scooter	
aeroplane	
ambulance	
helicopter	
hovercraft	

1 Write the correct word by each picture.

(1) ____________

(2) ____________

(3) ____________

(4) ____________

(5) ____________

(6) ____________

(7) ____________

(8) ____________

2 Add letters to each of these words to make words from the list.

(1) _ u s

(2) _ _ g i n _

(3) _ o v e r _ _ _ _ _

(4) _ _ _ _ l a n c e

(5) _ a n

(6) _ c o o t _ _

(7) r o c k _ _

(8) _ r a i n

(9) _ _ _ _ p l a n _

Look, cover and then write.

knit	____	comb	____	wrong	____
know	____	lamb	____	write	____
knock	____	climb	____	thumb	____
knife	____	crumb	____	autumn	____

What do you notice when you say the words out loud?

1 Circle the letter in each word which is not sounded.

knit	____	lamb	____	knock	____
comb	____	know	____	wrong	____
write	____	crumb	____	thumb	____

2 Write the correct word on each dotted line.

1 ____

2 tiny piece of bread ____

3 to make a garment with needles ____

4 to strike (a door) ____

5 to put words on paper ____

6 I ____ how to spell

7 $2 + 3 = 6$ This sum is ____

8 ____

9 the third season ____

10 to ____ a ladder

11 ____

12 ____

There are no rules about silent consonants. Each word must be learnt separately. On this page are some of the more common words of this kind that children are likely to meet.

Look/Cover	Write
goal	
cricket	
golf	
football	
hockey	
captain	
soccer	
badminton	
jersey	
tennis	
netball	
rugby	
squash	
amateur	

1 Write the names of eight ball games into this puzzle. If your answers are correct, the down column will give the name of a ninth game.

1 c
2 f
3 g
4 t
5 b
6 k
7 y
8 c

2 Mixed Up Dan's spelling is getting better! Instead of jumbling all the letters in a word, he now mixes up only those in the middle (e.g. for hockey, he writes hcokey). Can you sort out these sporting words for him?

(1) foboatll ____________ (3) nebatll ____________ (5) capatin ____________

(2) roduners ____________ (4) jseery ____________ (6) amteaur ____________

Look, cover and then write.

catch ________ watch ________ patch ________ scratch ________

pitch ________ witch ________ ditch ________ switch ________

match ________ fetch ________ hutch ________ satchel ________

1 Write the word from the list which fits each clue.

(1) Games are played on it. ________

(2) Water runs along it. ________

(3) It is made by a sharp point. ________

(4) A bag for books ________

(5) To go to get something ________

(6) To grab and hold on ________

2 Choose and write the correct word to fit each picture.

The group of words on this page all contain the letter string 'tch'. The first exercise tests knowledge of meanings as well as spellings.

Look/ Cover	Write
father	
mother	
sister	
Sunday	
Monday	
Tuesday	
Wednesday	
Thursday	
Friday	
Saturday	
night	
plastic	
yesterday	

1 Complete this programme of sports events by adding the names of the days of the week. Cover the list.

Sunday	July 1st	Marathon
______	July 2nd	Gymnastics
______	July 3rd	Swimming Finals
______	July 4th	Cricket
______	July 5th	Athletics
______	July 6th	School Sports
______	July 7th	Cycle Race

2 Use the words which are **not** names of days of the week to fill the spaces in these sentences.

I went to the Sports last (1) ______ and met Jack and his (2) ______, Mr Owen. Kathie, Jack's youngest (3) ______, was in the 100 metre sprint. Mrs Owen, Jack's (4) ______ was afraid that Kathie would catch cold. It poured with rain most of (5) ______ and Mrs Owen was grumbling at Kathie because she would not run in her (6) ______ mac!

hide	make	ride	take	save	drive
↓	↓	↓	↓	↓	↓
hiding	making	riding	taking	saving	driving

1 Fill each space in this story with the '__ ing' form of one of the words above.

Tim was (1) __________ in the hedge when he saw the highwaymen (2)

(2) __________ by. They were on their way to hold up the coach as it was

(3) __________ through the wood. After (4) __________ the people get down

from the coach, the highwaymen intended (5) __________ their money and

jewels. Tim knew what he had to do. By stopping the coach and

(6) __________ the rich people from being robbed, he could earn a good

reward. He set off along the road to warn the driver, running as fast as he

could go.

2 Write the '__ ing' form of each of these words.

(1) bite __________ (3) name __________ (5) rake __________

(2) type __________ (4) race __________ (6) dive __________

Hide → hiding. To form the -ing form of a verb ending in 'e', the final 'e' is dropped. When the child has worked through the exercises, try together to think of other verbs of this kind.

Look, cover and then write.

shirt	______	denim	______	jeans	______
skirt	______	fibre	______	fabric	______
cotton	______	ribbon	______	scarf	______
dungarees	______	uniform	______	sweater	______

Complete this crossword puzzle with words from the list. The clues are all pictures.

1 Write these words in:

	small letters	capitals
sale	______	______
open	______	______
danger	______	______
closed	______	______
entrance	______	______
exit	______	______
hotel	______	______
garage	______	______
school	______	______

2 Write one of the first five words, **in capitals,** to fill each space on these notices.

3 Write one of the last four words into each space in these sentences.

Dad drops me off at (1) ______ on his way to work every morning.

Every (2) ______ must have a clearly marked fire (3) ______

On Fridays, the car salesman at the (4) ______ works late.

The words in the list are familiar because they are often seen – written in capital letters – on street signs. The exercises give practice in writing the words in both capital and small letters.

Look, cover and then write.

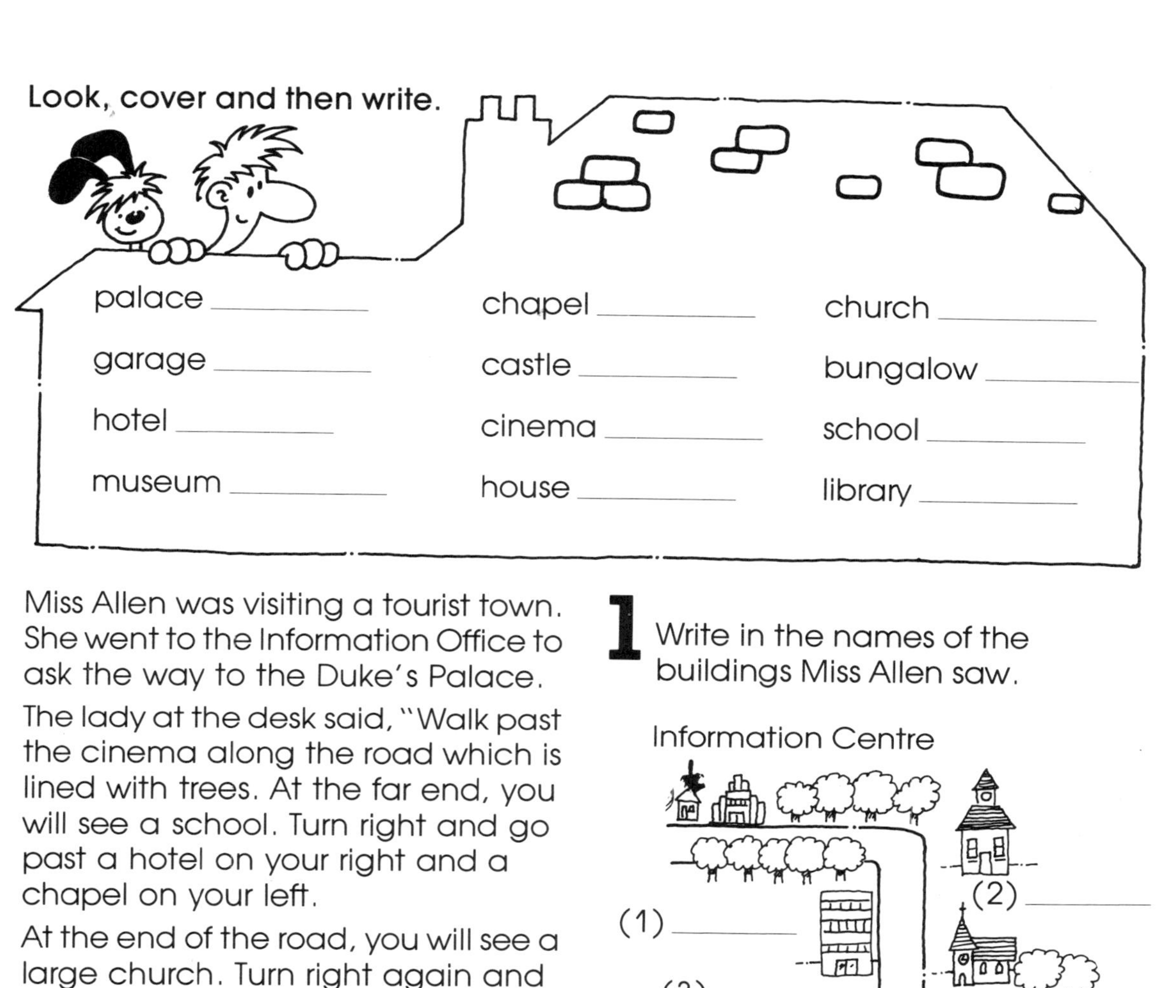

Miss Allen was visiting a tourist town. She went to the Information Office to ask the way to the Duke's Palace.

The lady at the desk said, "Walk past the cinema along the road which is lined with trees. At the far end, you will see a school. Turn right and go past a hotel on your right and a chapel on your left.

At the end of the road, you will see a large church. Turn right again and you will see a garage on a corner. Turn left there and you will soon see a lake with a castle at the far end. You will find the palace opposite the castle."

1 Write in the names of the buildings Miss Allen saw.

2 Write words from the list into the frames to complete these two puzzles.

1			p		
2			e		
3			a		
4			r		

Learn these words and their plurals.

leaf – leaves	loaf – loaves	scarf – scarves	thief – thieves
elf – elves	half – halves	shelf – shelves	sheaf – sheaves
wolf – wolves	calf – calves		

Learn these important exceptions.

roof – roofs gulf – gulfs reef – reefs chief – chiefs dwarf – dwarfs

1

Take letters from the end of the first word and from the beginning of the second to form a word ending in __f. Write the word and its plural.

Example: Marshal forgiven→half→halves

(1) local farmers

(2) travel freely

(3) whole afternoon

(4) solo afterwards

2

Find a word in the two lists above to match each picture. Write the plural of the word into the frame. If your answers are correct, the dotted space will enclose the plural of a noun beginning with 'f'.

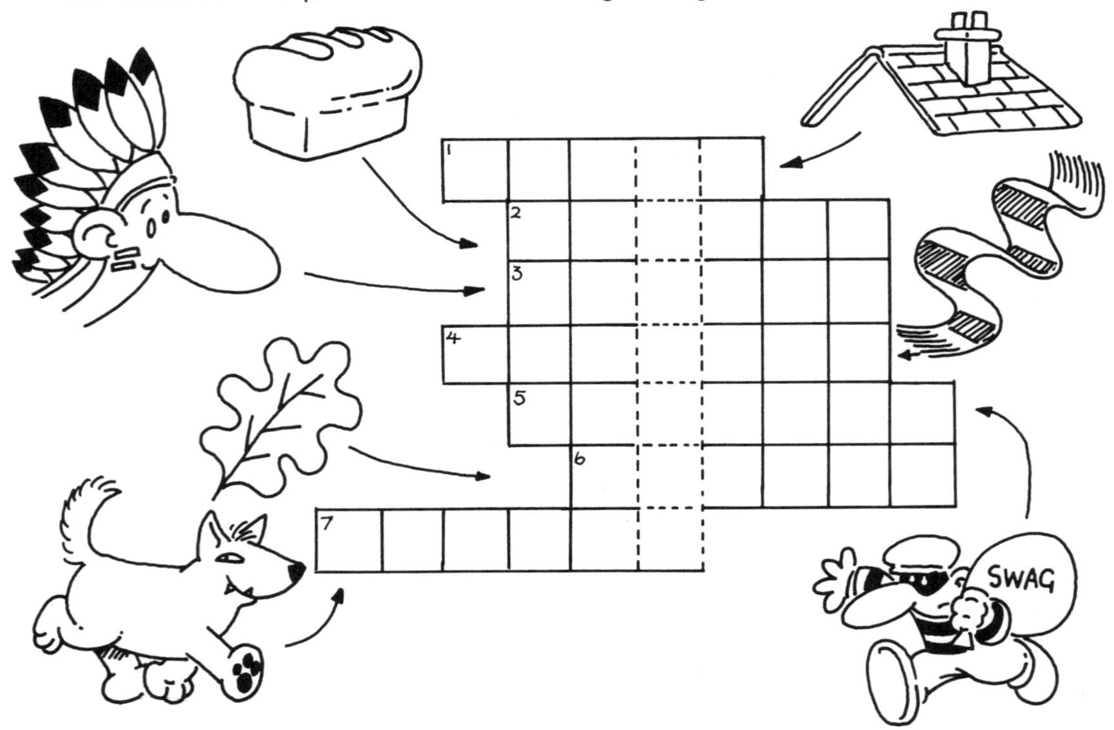

Look/Cover/Write	Look	Write again	√ or self correct
onion ______			
radio ______			
violin ______			
million ______	1000,000		
station ______			
violet ______			
fashion ______			
chariot ______			
stallion ______			
television ______			

1 The four rules of number are called addition, subtraction, division and multiplication. Write the correct word by each sign.

+ (1) ______ ÷ (2) ______ − (3) ______ × (4) ______

2 Add the letters 'i' and 'o' to complete each of these words. Say each word and find out what it means.

(1) n a t _ _ n (2) t r _ _ (3) c u r _ _ u s (4) g l o r _ _ u s

(5) k _ _ s k

The group of words on this page all contain the letter string 'io'. Try and see if the child can think of other words with the 'io' letter string.

Look/Cover	Write
ruby	
diamond	
emerald	
gold	
silver	
sapphire	
pearl	
bracelet	
necklace	
brooch	
pendant	
jewellery	

1 Write words from the list into these brooch frames. You will need five words for the upper frame and four for the lower one.

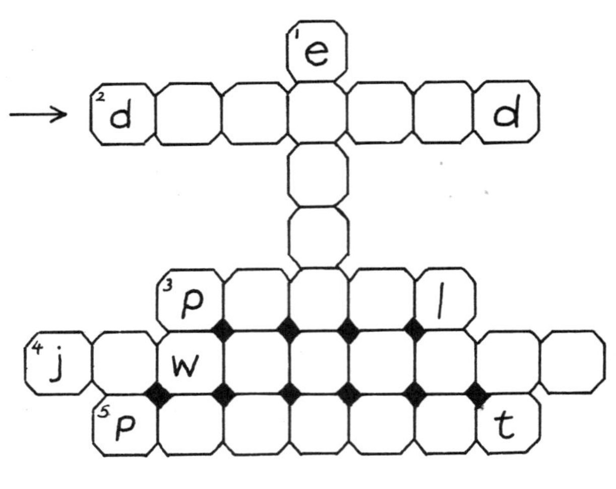

2 Mixed Up Dan is having trouble again. Can you help him to sort out these words from the list?

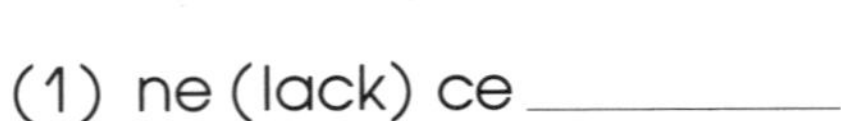

(1) ne (lack) ce ____________

(2) br (lace) et ____________

(3) pe (and) nt ____________

(4) d (Naomi) d ____________

(5) s (live) r ____________

(6) e (realm) d ____________

(7) p (are) l ____________

Answers

Page 3
2 (1) who (2) was (3) made (4) what (5) came

Page 4
1 (1) before (2) were (3) could (4) said (5) little
'Fruit' grows on the tree.
2 (1) which (2) little (3) before (4) were

Page 5
2 (1) Our (2) went (3) like (4) where (5) only (6) other (7) want (8) when (9) One (10) with

Page 6
(1) shorts (2) fort (3) anorak (4) mirror (5) fork (6) corgi (7) sword (8) north

Page 7
(1) read (2) hear (3) beak (4) meat (5) seal (6) bean

Page 8
1 (1) badger (2) camel (3) panda (4) lion
2 (1) bear (2) giraffe (3) badger (4) tiger (5) leopard
3 (1) wolf (2) rabbit (3) monkey (4) elephant

Page 9
2 **Across** (1) black (3) brown (8) green (10) lemon (12) white (14) cream
Down (4) red

Page 10
2 (1) wood (2) sore (3) knew (4) would (5) bored (6) new
Pictures (1) hare (2) wood (3) flower

Page 11
2 (1) drawer (2) metre (3) weigh (4) road (5) draw (6) tyre (7) rode (8) meter

Page 12
1 (1) orange (2) cherry (3) pea (4) apple (5) carrot (6) peach (7) potato (8) pineapple (9) grape (10) cabbage (11) banana (12) plum
2 (1) plum (2) peach (3) cherry (4) grape
3 **Down** (4) peach **Across** (8) orange (9) potato (10) grape (11) banana (12) cherry

Page 13
1 (1) buses (2) taxes (3) classes (4) crosses (5) bushes (6) foxes (7) churches (8) patches
2 (1) women (2) dresses (3) patches (4) branches (5) witches (6) wishes (7) boxes (8) bushes (9) cards (10) Tricks

Page 14
(1) caravan (2) farm (3) arm (4) garden (5) car (6) bark

Page 15
1 (1) ice-cream (2) bread (3) milk (4) chocolate (5) sausages (6) biscuit (7) cheese (8) hamburger
2 (1) biscuit (2) coffee (3) potato (4) bread (5) ice-cream (6) hamburger (7) milk (8) pizza (9) chips (10) chocolate (11) sausages (12) cheese

Page 16
(1) slapped, slapping (2) gripped, gripping (3) chatted, chatting (4) snipped, snipping

Page 18
2 (1) puppies (2) collies (3) babies (4) toys (5) mysteries (6) cherries (7) pansies (8) daisies (9) days (10) ladies (11) puppies (12) sties

Page 19
1 (1) van (2) aeroplane (3) helicopter (4) train (5) rocket (6) truck (7) ambulance (8) bus
2 (1) bus (2) engine (3) hovercraft (4) ambulance (5) van (6) scooter (7) rocket (8) train (9) aeroplane

Page 20
1 knit, comb, write, lamb, know, crumb, knock, wrong, thumb
2 (1) comb (2) crumb (3) knit (4) knock (5) write (6) know (7) wrong (8) lamb (9) autumn (10) climb (11) knife (12) thumb

Page 21
1 (1) cricket (2) golf (3) squash (4) tennis (5) badminton (6) hockey (7) rugby (8) soccer
2 (1) football (2) rounders (3) netball (4) jersey (5) captain (6) amateur

Page 22
1 (1) pitch (2) ditch (3) scratch (4) satchel (5) fetch (6) catch
2 (1) switch (2) patch (3) hutch (4) witch (5) match

Page 23
2 (1) night (2) father (3) sister (4) mother (5) yesterday (6) plastic

Page 24
1 (1) hiding (2) riding (3) driving (4) making (5) taking (6) saving
2 (1) biting (2) typing (3) naming (4) racing (5) raking (6) diving

Page 25

Across (1) skirt (2) ribbon (3) fabric (4) dungarees (5) shirt (6) jeans (7) uniform (8) sweater

Page 26

2 (1) ENTRANCE (2) OPEN (3) CLOSED (4) SALE (5) DANGER

3 (1) school (2) hotel (3) exit (4) garage

Page 27

1 (1) cinema (2) school (3) hotel (4) chapel (5) church (6) garage (7) castle (8) palace

2 (1) chapel (2) cinema (3) garage (4) church (5) palace (6) library (7) bungalow (8) museum

Page 28

1 (1) calf, calves (2) elf, elves (3) leaf, leaves (4) loaf, loaves

2 (1) roofs (2) loaves (3) chiefs (4) scarves (5) thieves (6) leaves (7) wolves

New word: fairies

Page 29

1 (1) addition (2) division (3) substraction (4) multiplication

2 (1) nation (2) trio (3) curious (4) glorious (5) kiosk

Page 30

1 (1) emerald (2) diamond (3) pearl (4) jewellery (5) pendant (6) ruby (7) bracelet (8) necklace (9) gold

2 (1) necklace (2) bracelet (3) pendant (4) diamond (5) silver (6) emerald (7) pearl